Freedom from Debt:

A Simple Guide

By Es Westmoreland

Freedom from Debt

Cover design by Kellie Southerland (Previous ISBN: 978-1-61663-204-5)

Unless otherwise noted, all Scriptures are from the New International Version.

Published in the United States of America

ISBN: 978-0-9988361-1-9
Business & Economics: Personal Finance: General
10.03.30

Dedication

To everyone who has made my life so rich and free, especially my husband, Frank, our wonderful children; their spouses; and our terrific grandchildren.

Also, to my six brothers and sisters with whom I shared my young life in Michigan. They also love the Lord, and have kept our love for one another burning bright. May God richly bless you.

FORWARD

Es Westmoreland is a remarkable Christian lady. As her husband for some 46 years I am continually amazed by her non-stop unveiling of talents, abilities, and desire to help others.

When we married, she was immediately thrown into life as the wife of a career U. S. Army officer – a lifelong on experiences but short on cash! Four short months later I deployed for a one year unaccompanied tour in the Republic of Korea. Her response was to return home to Michigan, go to work, and help her widowed Mother and family any way she could.

Over the ensuing years, Es brought three sons and a daughter into the world while moving often. Regardless of location, she immediately immersed herself into helping others however she could. Throughout, she regularly attended Church and normally taught one or more Sunday School classes.

As my later military assignments became longer in duration, Es found time to perform more visible positions in Church while also attending Bible study meetings. When we moved to Houston for what became my final military assignment, Es was fully immersed in Youth Group activities while raising our teen-aged children.

By then our oldest son was a in his first year at Texas A & M and cash was becoming a problem as we contemplated the college educations for the remaining three at home. Her response was quick – she returned to secretarial duties after many years away and immediately dazzled everyone with the organizational skills and no-nonsense attitude she brought to the workplace.

When my Mother died and my blind Father needed a home, she quit her job, took him in, and exposed him to prayer and the Bible for the first time in his adult life. After two long difficult years of her daily ministering to him, he invited the Lord Jesus Christ to take charge of his life when he was 88 years old.

Not surprisingly she was ordained in the work of the Gospel Ministry in 1990! She has functioned as an Associate Pastor at Eastgate Church in Dayton, Texas ever since.

This book is designed to help anyone who is looking for quick, simple, and understandable ways to start getting out of the financial hole they are in. Unfortunately, it also demands a burning desire to change and the personal discipline to take the first step to make a change! We did it and so can you – right now on this day!

Franklin D. Westmoreland (Colonel, US Army, Retired)

Table of Contents

INTRODUCTION

During her adult years, Es Westmoreland has taken many financial classes, gone to seminars, and read many books to try to get an understanding of how money works. She has read the Bible many times and has become familiar with God's promises and his desire for us to prosper.

Es became aware that some people do not save, because they either do not understand compound interest, or do not think they have any extra money to save—not realizing that even five dollars a month is a start point.

Others do not use their company's retirement plan, because they think that you have to have a lot of money to participate.

Through it all, she has gotten a basic understanding of some things to do and some things to avoid. Presented here are possible strategies to inform you about money and to help you understand that money either works for you or against you.

If even one or two of these strategies make sense, they can help you reclaim some of your hard-earned money so you can be debt free and enjoy life to the fullest!

Freedom from Debt:

A Simple Guide

Sometime near the end of two wonderful weeks visiting her son and daughter-in-law in Singapore, Es read an interesting article in the local newspaper. A reporter had written about religion, describing the change between the 1980 census and the 1990 census.

He found that not only was Christianity rising, but also that the income of Christians increased over the general population. Over the next few days, she mulled over the various reasons that might be causing this.

The trip home from Singapore included a three-day layover in Hawaii. Because of flying through many time zones, she was awake in the middle of the night thinking about this financial difference. She then began merging the information she had learned from the Bible with her knowledge of other sources about saving money.

Obviously, she needed to write this information down, or it would sink back into oblivion. Turning on a small light, she began to write, and the basis for this book was captured.

As a Beginning

Since this book was written for you, let's get right to the heart of the matter. Ask yourself these questions:

Do you earn or receive as much money as you need? The Bible states in II Corinthians 9:8,

> "And God is able to make all grace abound to you, so that in all things at all times, having all that you need, you will abound in every good work."

Are you better off financially now than you were before you got saved? The passage in II Corinthians 8:9 states,

> "For you know the grace of our Lord Jesus Christ, that though he was rich, yet for your sakes he became poor, so that you through his poverty might become rich."

Additionally, there are many more promises concerning your financial well-being given in the Bible. Philippians 4:19 says,

> "And my God will meet all your needs according to his glorious riches in Christ Jesus."

God has pledged himself to help you prosper if you are his child. God's plan for your life is that you have adequate finances so your needs may be met. To prove this to be true in your case, please review Ephesians 3:20,

> "Now to him who is able to do immeasurably more than we ask or imagine, according to his power that is at work within us."

Also consider III John 2,

> "Dear Friend, I pray that you may enjoy good health and that all may go well with you, even as your soul is getting along well."

In KJV, it reads:

> *"Beloved, I wish above all things that thou mayest prosper and be in health, even as thy soul prospereth."*

The only requirement that God puts on his followers in the area of finance is found in Malachi 3-10

> "Will a man rob God? Yet you rob me. But you ask, How do we rob you? In tithes and offerings. You are under a curse -- the whole nation of you -- because you are robbing me. Bring the whole tithe into the storehouse, that there may be food in my house. Test me in this, says the Lord mighty and see if I will not throw open the floodgates of heaven and pour out so much blessing that you will not have room enough for it."

Some say that tithing was done away with in the New Testament, but if you look closely, tithing is also in the New Testament according to Matthew 23:23,

> "Woe to you, teachers of the law and Pharisees, you hypocrites! You give a tenth of your spices -- mint, dill and cumin. But you have neglected the more important matters of the law -- justice, mercy and faithfulness. You should have practiced the latter without neglecting the former."

Also, Hebrews 7:8 says,

> "In the one case, the tenth is collected by men who die; but in the other case, by him who is declared to be living."

God's plan of tithing is not to take your hard-earned money, but that you give God something to work with so he may bless you according to his plan for your financial abundance. Since he has ordained tithing as well as giving, he works within this framework as recorded in the Bible.

God also requests love offerings. These are gifts from the heart that he works to produce the thirty, sixty, or one hundred-fold return. After that, he gives clear instructions about what to do (and what not to do) with money while alerting us to stay away from "get-rich-quick" schemes. When we "go our own way" and depart from the Bible, we quickly find that we "go it alone."

Tithing not only opens the windows of heaven, but God also rebukes the devourer for us. Malachi 3:11-12 says,

> "I will prevent pests from devouring your crops, and the vines in your fields will not cast their fruit, says the Lord Almighty. Then all the nations will call you blessed, for yours will be a delightful land, says the Lord Almighty."

Once married, the very first decision Es and her husband made was to tithe on their gross income (before taxes) from all sources. They mistakenly assumed that God would automatically rebuke the devourer. Even though God kept them and took care of them, they called the repairman or bought new just like everyone else when something broke down.

Their Pastor began teaching about tithing and giving in a very special and unique way. When presenting tithes and offerings in church, they would hold their envelope up and repeat Malachi 3:10-11.

They came to realize that, just as in the Scriptures concerning salvation and healing, they had a part to play in causing these Scriptures to function. They found they had to pray about the situation and then stand in faith on God's word. From that time on, when something broke, they reminded God of what he said in his Word and asked him to either fix it supernaturally or show them how to handle the situation.

Sometimes it was just Satan jamming his finger into appliances or in the car's mechanism. Other times, it truly needed repair or replacement, and they asked God to make a way so the devil couldn't steal their finances or peace of mind.

In all instances, God revealed himself to be wonderfully faithful. Sometimes he repaired the car, the washer, the dryer and many other things himself when they laid hands on them and asked God to heal them. Other times, he provided an alternative way. God transformed seemingly impossible problems into minor ones that were then inexpensively resolved.

Remember how Jesus handled the tax issue by sending Peter fishing? Matthew 17:27 states,

> "But so that we may not offend them, go to the lake and throw out your line. Take the first fish you catch; open its mouth and you will find a four-drachma coin. Take it and give it to them for my tax and yours."

Jesus will make a way for you. Is he any different today than he was then? The answer is clearly, *no!* Hebrews 13:8 says,

> "Jesus Christ the same yesterday, and today and forever."

Plan Your Financial Work -Work Your Financial Plan

The following Scripture was a turning point for Es. Proverbs 27:23-27 says,

> "Be sure you know the condition of your flocks, give attention to your herds; for riches do not endure forever, and a crown is not secure for all generations. When the hay is removed and new growth appears and the grass from the hills is gathered in, the lambs will provide you with clothing, and the goats with the price of a field. You will have plenty of goats' milk to feed you and your family and to nourish your servant girls."

Like many of you, Es lives in a subdivision. So for her, God wasn't talking about livestock, but about finances. In Proverbs 2:1-6, she discovered that strategies provide solutions to difficult problems.

> "My son, if you accept my words and store up my commands within you, turning your ear to wisdom and applying your heart to understanding, and if you call out for insight and cry aloud for understanding and if you look for it as for silver and search for it as for hidden treasure, then you will understand the fear of the Lord and find the knowledge of God. For the Lord gives wisdom and from his mouth come knowledge and understanding."

God has given us help in gaining knowledge about our finances. The passage in I Corinthians 12:28 shows us this.

> "And in the church God has appointed first of all apostles, second prophets, third teachers, then workers of miracles, also those having gifts of healing, those able to help others, those with gifts of administration, and those speaking in different kinds of tongues."

There are four powerful men who have written books that make God's financial principles clear. They are John Avanzini, Larry Burkett, Gerald Davis, and Dave Ramsey. They are strong, Bible-based teachers with a mandate from God to show us how to get out of debt and prosper.

Proverbs 24:3-4 says,

> "By wisdom a house is built, and through understanding it is established; through knowledge its rooms are filled with rare and beautiful treasures."

The information these men present is a breath of fresh air on a stale, gruesome, strife-causing, anger-producing, and gridlocked situations. Unchecked, this strife destroys the very fiber that holds marriages and businesses together. God has revealed truth in Scripture that radically differs from the world's system. Always remember, God is for you!

The previously mentioned men have solid, conservative methods that seem "ho-hum" to many and are not instantly gratifying. They don't advocate praying down a million dollars to end your financial woes so you can live happily ever after. They force you to get a grip on that stampeding horse of debt and bring him under control.

Budget: Facing Where My Money Went

The starting point is to know the Scriptures, and it is also important to do your part so God can do the supernatural. You must create a spending plan to direct your money to specific needs and savings.

This plan is not fun to prepare. Coming face-to-face with your financial picture isn't comfortable but it is the only way you can see where you are financially. Create a budget that includes the tithe and savings for your current income.

Most people realize too late that they have over-spent in one or more category while other necessities are left out. In this case, you must redo your budget to reflect what your real needs.

Some Financial Strategies That Won't Work

Often people dream of suddenly receiving windfall cash from "old Uncle Jake" to solve their money problems. Ecclesiastes 10:19 says,

> "A feast is made for laughter, and wine makes life merry, but money is the answer for everything."

One tempting way out of financial dilemmas is to transfer money from one bank account to another while trying to keep ahead of hot checks (it's called kiting.) This strategy is stress filled, will not work, and will blow up in your face eventually. The usual solution is always "more money."

Don't incur debt and then think someone will bail you out. Your blessings from God should be "fair and square." It is possible that someone, out of the goodness of their heart, will come and catch you up on your bills. This is "miracle money," but you cannot reasonably expect others to pay your way. God says in Romans 13:8,

> "Let no debt remain outstanding, except the continuing debt to love one another, for he who loves his fellowman has fulfilled the law."

Unfortunately, unless you radically change your spending habits, the windfall of "miracle money" will get used up, and you will be right back in the same deep financial mess you were before!

Reality: Bottom Line

The cold hard truth is that we need to work, earn, tithe, give, share with others, and expect God to be God in every part of our lives. If you have a financial need, let work provide for it instead of borrowing. If need be, take an extra job (or jobs) to obtain cash. Apply your God-given talents to bake pies, make craft items, mow yards, deliver pizza or do whatever you can to earn extra money. As you work, always give value. As you earn more, don't forget to tithe on it and report your additional income on your taxes.

If you are absolutely desperate for funds and cannot earn quickly enough, sell something. Don't be too proud to undo the damage! The result of being financially free is well worth the short-term pain that results in being emotionally and financially at peace.

In Daniel 6:4, he was examined by the others to see if they could find any fault or error in him. The Bible says they could not find one thing out of order.

> "At this, the administrators and the satraps tried to find grounds for charges against Daniel in his conduct of government affairs, but they were unable to do so."

Be a Daniel!

The Truth About Credit Card Debt

We live at a time when credit card spending seems to be the preferred way to purchase everything. People feel wealthy when they can flash a card rather than counting out cash. Also, people go into debt to build a "credit rating," thinking the more debt they have, the higher score they will have. This is a huge trap because when you build up large debt, your credit score goes down, and you couldn't get a loan if you wanted to.

Credit card debt is choking our families both young and old. Not surprisingly, little babies arrive with all kinds of little needs, middle-sized kids have middle-sized needs, and big kids go to college. By the time children arrive at college age, they have big tastes and plans for the way they would like to live while still on Mom and Dad's payroll. If there's no taste of reality developed, they will eventually graduate from college with monumental debt from student loans that seemed like such a lifesaver at the time, but have now become an albatross hanging around their neck.

It is imperative that you teach your children at an early age to work, while also teaching them how to make and manage money, so they can live independently and well.

The best financial guide will always be the Bible. Matthew 6:33 KJV

> "But seek ye first the kingdom of God, and his righteousness; and all these things shall be added unto you."

Especially read and study the wonderful book of Proverbs in the Bible. Determine to get God's plan by praying to him and including him as partner in your finances. Salvation is a covenant with him, remember? He's on your side and desires that your needs be met in Christ Jesus! God will help you.

A Great Financial Strategy that Gets You out of Debt

Dave Ramsey has a wonderful way to pay off credit card debt with his "Debt Snowball." With his permission, I include his strategy. You pay minimums on all debts except the one with the fewest payments remaining—not the one with the highest interest rate. By selling "stuff" and working extra jobs, you put all the extra cash you can muster against that one debt and pay it off quickly.

Once that debt is paid, take the amount of that monthly payment and add it to the minimum payment of the next bill with the fewest payments remaining and pay it off. Each time you pay off a debt, add all of the previous payment amounts together and attack the next debt.

Of course, however, you must continue paying the minimums on all remaining debts. This will tremendously shorten the time you are in debt!

We all know that the farther you get into debt, the longer it takes to get out. There is a way out *if* you will stop charging. (If you don't stop, you will lose what you do have.) Remember the old joke: "How do you keep a bull from charging? Take away his credit card!"

Visualize what it will be like for you to be debt free and have money saved. That vision should change your whole outlook on life and energize you to get to that place.

Determine that you would rather work harder to get out of debt than to stay in the pain that debt causes. There is such joy in being debt free!

Some Financial Decisions You Must Make

Changing your spending habits will require new decisions. Getting out of debt means no impulse spending.

- *No cash* means no new "delight," such as the large screen TV until you have saved and can pay cash for it.
- *No cash* means no new paint for the dining room until you have it in the bank.
- *No cash* means no eating out! Truthfully, eating out takes a big slice out of your budget but gives no lasting return. In your budget, money for restaurants should never be included in the grocery money. It should be separately labeled or included in entertainment or recreation, because it's so uncontrollable.

Always take some time to decide about a major purchase by walking away. Very few purchases are life threatening. Breathe and wait. You may be able to find the same item at a garage sale or a resale shop at a fraction of the retail cost.

Once you have made your financial plan to get out of debt, you must also determine to live within your income.

Save for big purchases! There will always be telephone calls and letters offering you more credit cards. You will have to toughen up and say *no*—not even *no thanks!*

It is also recommended that you spend some "hard-earned" cash to buy one or more books by the previously mentioned authors to turn your financial picture around. The advice will work for you *if* you will not only put it to work, but discipline yourself to continue working it. Like a diet, it's only effective if you fully participate. The following are some strategies that will make it easier for your plans to work.

Control Spending by Balanced Billing

One very helpful method to control your spending is to qualify for balanced billing with your utility and insurance companies. You pay a standard monthly rate year-round, and they recalculate your usage once a year.

Your electric bill may seem high at the low usage periods of the year, but this becomes a wonderful "gift" at peak season when everyone else's bill is wiping them out, and you are within budget and staying peaceful.

Specialized Savings

Most Christians know the formula of giving 10% to God and spending 90%. Try a new approach to finance—instead of "frittering away" the 90%, save another 10% for retirement and set another 10% aside for future purchases. Using your accrued cash to buy what you need stops future credit card debt after you've finally paid it off using the "Debt Snowball" plan.

Go ahead, name ten items that you would buy with fifty dollars—maybe several fifties put together. Keep a list of future purchases you need or desire: gifts, household items, recreation, vacations, investments, etc., and rank them in order. When you have enough set aside for that next purchase, go ahead and buy it without ever again wondering how to pay for it.

Meet Infrequent Expenses through Targeted Savings

Normally credit cards are used to buy things you have no way of paying for at the moment such as birthdays, vacations, school clothing, Christmas presents and taxes. Planned savings will enable you to take care of these big, once a year expenses as they come up.

Make an estimate of the costs of all these non-monthly expenses. Divide the total by twelve and you will know how much you need to set aside each month to pay them. Your first year of this process will require lots of ingenuity, flexibility, and discipline.

Once you have firmly established this form of financial planning, the money will be available when you need it.

Use Payroll Deductions

One way of accruing special or yearly savings would be to establish payroll deductions that transfer funds to specified accounts through your employer. When enough money has been accumulated, transfer it into your checking account and write a check for the annual expense.

If you faithfully save money on autopilot, you will have adequate funds for once a year bills and big-ticket items.

Since there are generally no restrictions on the number of payroll deductions you can have, use separate savings accounts for each item. Cash, and only cash, buying is wonderfully freeing!

Plan for Retirement through Savings

You must have a plan for retirement. Health statistics show that life spans have extended into the eighties and nineties. There are several strategies to make this nearly painless.

One of the wonderful things about savings or some investment accounts is that they earn compound interest. This increases your money, because you earn interest the first year on your principle; the next year that interest is added to the principle and becomes the new principle, and you earn interest on the new total. It accumulates that way year after year and grows greatly over a number of years. This is especially important for retirement savings.

Warning: As it grows, it could be tempting to view it as your emergency account, but you *must not* touch it.

As an example, if you were to put one hundred dollars a month (or $1,200 a year) into a bank savings account that earned 4% *compound* interest for forty years (age 25-65 for retirement), you would not just have the $48,000 you put in but would have accumulated principal plus interest in the approximate amount of $118,102. This illustrates the "miracle" of compound interest. There are many other investment opportunities that offer higher rates of interest. You must research and decide what will work for you.

Think what your retirement savings would look like if you were able to put in more than $100 each month or at a higher rate of return. To show different possibilities, there are several internet websites you can visit to calculate the effect of different percentages. (www.bankrate.com is a sample.) Compound interest starts slowly, but you will see that it becomes a wealth snowball as the years fly by.

Plan for Retirement through Company Savings Plans

Company savings plans are yet another way to supercharge your retirement savings. Some employers have 401-k plans. These plans accumulate your savings before they take taxes out of your paycheck.

Many companies also match a certain percentage of your monthly savings. Often this "match" is in company stock, which fluctuates with the market price, but it can also pay dividends for reinvestment purposes providing a good snowball. 401-k (pre-tax) and Roth IRA (after the taxes have been taken out) savings plans are designed for retirement savings when you will no longer draw a regular paycheck.

This money should not be touched until you are at least fifty-nine and a half. At the time of withdrawal from your 401-k, the money will be taxed at the regular rate while Roth withdrawals are not because you have already paid tax on it. If you withdraw from your 401-k before you are fifty-nine and a half, be aware it will be taxed at the regular rate *plus* a big penalty.

Protect Your Family: Buy Term Life Insurance

Another important item is Level Term Life insurance. It can provide a large sum of money for your family at an extremely low cost if you were to die early. Term policies vary in length, possibly for as long as twenty years. The younger you are at the time of purchase, the lower the premium. The usual amount to purchase is ten times your annual income. If wisely invested at ten percent, the insurance money could give your family about the same income as before.

It is important to make wise decisions on all insurance.

As an example, calculate the difference in premium cost for term and whole life to determine what you could do with the cost savings if it were invested during the policy's duration.

You may only need term insurance while your children are growing, becoming self-insured after that by investing the difference. At the end of the initial term length, you could buy a new policy with increased premiums to create an estate for your family. You may also need whole life insurance.

Protect Your Family: Get a Will

Pay the money and consult an attorney for correct wording of a will that designates how you want your estate to be distributed.

If you die "intestate" (without a will), your estate will use some of the money you intended to leave to your family to pay other fees. Be wise—get a will and review it on an annual basis.

Summary

The above strategies are set forth to help you rise up and become commander of your own finances. God has set you on high and desires that you prosper in every arena.

Being out of debt will actually save you money. You will not have to pay finance charges nor have the hassle or cost of credit bill paying each month. Once you decide to get out of debt and implement the plan to do so, you will be in charge of your life rather than having the charges in your life dictating what you can or cannot do.

If you have never experienced being debt free, you have wonderful freedom awaiting you. Don't shortcut your payments, and don't try to stick someone else with your bill. *Pray*, obey the Bible in tithing and giving, and use every available legal and moral way to get out of debt. If you have children, teach them how to live debt free too.

Welcome to a new, debt-free life, and may God richly bless you!

Prayer for Your Finances

Dear Father, in the mighty name of Jesus Christ, I come before You and ask You to help restore financial freedom to me and my family. Through lack of knowledge, I have either gotten myself into debt or am not as financially free as you want me to be. I believe III John 2 with all of my heart that You desire for me to prosper and be in health even as my soul prospers. Help me learn about finances so that my soul prospers in knowledge. Show me what corrections to make. Help me to tithe and give into Your Kingdom. I commit myself to Your way of doing things. Thank You in advance for your help and guidance. In Jesus' name, Amen.

Bibliography

John Avanzini, *"War on Debt" – Breaking the Power of Debt,"* Financial Freedom Series, Vol 1, Ft. Worth, TX , HIS Publishing Company, 1990.
ISBN 1-878605-00-3

Larry Burkett, *"Family Budgets That Work" – Pocket Guide,"* Wheaton, IL, Tyndale House Publishers, Inc, 1988.
ISBN 0-8423-0829-6

Gerald W. Davis, *"How to Function in this Economy According to Heaven's Economy,"* Coppell, Texas, FAME Publishing, Incorporated, 1994.
ISBN 1-880563-08-8

Dave Ramsey, *"Financial Peace Revisited,"* New York, NY, Viking, Published by the Penguin Group, 2003.
ISBN 0-670-03208-5 (Permission given)

Made in United States
Troutdale, OR
11/03/2026

56845118R00020